Printed in the United States of America

Prologue

Why this book?

> *I want to inspire future product managers (PMs) and entrepreneurs with a tangible toolkit that will ignite problem solving for humans.*

Anyone can be a PM and we are each empowered to solve human needs.

I have been a PM for over 15 years and I was an early pioneer with BT to build live and on-demand video capabilities at scale in the mid 2000's for the likes of MLB.tv, NYSE.com and Oscar.com (Academy Awards).

I have been a part of a number of startups and public/private companies working as a consultant, digital strategist, innovation lead, and group product manager.

Throughout my career, MBA education, and immersion in different problem solving methodologies I have gathered together a toolkit I want to share with other PMs and entrepreneurs. I especially want to inspire new PMs with the valuable lessons I have learned.

I want to challenge any perception that we can solve complex problems in silos or by ego-driven mentalities.

Collaborative teams and diverse cultures yield many infinite possibilities for our customers. We as PMs can help drive our teams to the most important possibilities.

If there is one thing I have learned then it is to bring out the best in people. I am giving you my best lessons in a concise way because,

Giving back has been immeasurably fulfilling to me as a product leader.

I hope the reader will be able to learn something from this toolkit and share their learnings as well.

Thank you for reading.

Table of Contents

What is Product Management?

Product Management is building to solve human needs.

As a PM, you are the owner or entrepreneur of a product(s).

You may have inherited the responsibilities of an existing product or have been assigned with coming up with a new product (or even a new industry). Empathy or imagining being in someone else's shoes helps PMs envision how customers may feel friction or pain points.

To take it one step further, Compassion or *activated empathy* is critical for PMs to cultivate the right solutions for customers.

Discipline allows PMs to organize what's important. We cultivate roadmaps, prioritize, and plan our work for the customer needs in a realistic way. Agile methods of working allow us to perform rituals that include daily and planning sessions for measurable outcomes we need to build together as a team. A PM works with a cross-functional team(s) to partner with to deliver value or solve problems. For digital PMs, this usually includes software developers, designers, and testers. A cross-functional team that genuinely challenges each other and collaborates well, will deliver meaningful value to the customer.

What is Design Thinking?

Design thinking is a method of problem solving that allows us to assess a problem and figure out potential solutions by hearing from customers directly.

The power of design thinking is the ability to feel firsthand the empathy for the customer, but it also allows us to gather first party data to uncover unmet needs.

Why do Product Managers need design thinking?

PM's use design thinking as it allows us to learn directly from our customers, to create space for strategic thinking, and to cultivate new unmet needs for our customers.

PMs may need to decide if their role is to provide ongoing enhancements, create new products, and/or create new opportunity spaces altogether.

UVA professor Jeanne Liedtka (2013) mentioned that in contrary to: "*traditional approaches to planning...excessive emphasis on numbers...*" that "*Design offers a different approach and suggests processes that are more widely participative, more dialogue-based, issue-rather than calendar-driven, and conflict-using...*".

One of the primary ways to conduct design thinking is to gather feedback from customers at extreme ends of the normal distribution curve or extreme personas of customers. Its working hypothesis is that these extreme customers have workarounds or other methods to solve for their needs.

For example, how might we learn from an extreme customer who only shops from CSA's or only grows their own food sources?

Based on your area of focus you can zoom out to identify the customers you could learn from to help solve problems.

Design Thinking allows PMs to zoom out from building small things to learn how to build bigger, innovative things.

What attitudes and behaviors do I need to embody as a PM?

To be a successful PM, there are a set of attitudes and behaviors which could ignite the best outcomes for the collective team. As with any profession, there are critical EQ related skills needed to maximize your potential as a PM. Also, let's not forget to insert a bit of fun as 'play' is an important aspect to learning. Also, people generally want to work with fun and pleasant folks (than the opposite).

Empathy

PMs need to immerse themselves in the shoes of the customer to proceed with developing meaningful solutions.

Deeper awareness or empathy for the customer can then activate compassion to build the right thing or solve for the right problem.

I challenge you to activate your empathy for something you are seeing right now.

What can you do to help someone who has a pain point? What can you learn from them on what they need?

Humility

Design thinking requires humility. The PM should discard all preconceived notions, biases or assumptions about what they think they know about the customer.

Being humble allows PMs to absorb and learn from customers and cross-functional team members.

There is a basic tool that Second City's Improv comedians use to build up the infectious possibilities of their troupe.

> *Building on each other's ideas using "Yes, and" (versus "No, but") is a powerful way to open up possibilities for brainstorming and ultimately product development.*

Listening

True listening to the customer requires ego to be set aside so that the friction and pain points of customers can be heard.

Active listening requires the PM to hear what is being said, note it down if possible, and also mirror back what is being heard. Mirroring customers will allow comfort for the customer to share more.

"Tell me more" is an easy way to encourage additional feedback.

Curiosity

PMs are insatiably curious about their customers. This means that PMs will benefit from crafting questions to better understand their customer.

Asking *"Why?"* and *"Tell Me More"* allows for more context and specificity of what is being conveyed by the customer. It is important not to lead the customer to get to true insights.

Problem solving is rooted in genuine curiosity. To learn meaningful customer insights, you have to be willing to go deeper into the conversation.

Asking why versus how is critical in getting to understanding the root problem at hand.

Bias awareness

Self-awareness and social awareness (Goleman and Boyatzis, 2017) are just some of the valuable EQ domains to note as a PM or any individual for that matter.

It is also important to be able to realize when you have cognitive biases. Some clues on this is if you were to make judgements about someone, some thing, some place and you keep sticking with that story even when presented with alternate evidence.

As with any story, there are multiple stories that can come from it and multiple perspectives.

Allowing openness to be receptive and observing things for what they are enables PM's to better discern inherent needs. Sticking with biases can introduce an ego-driven way of product development which serves no one, especially the customer.

Having an open mind and noticing when bias can affect judgement allows for exciting possibilities for product building.

Daring

PMs need a bit of daring to go after their passion products.

Tiny improvements are not usually what PMs are striving for.

We are capable of making change in the world.

A bit of courage and risk is needed to change or improve our collective human experience. Make sure to listen to those who have needs to empower your daring.

Creativity

One does not need a design degree to be a PM. However, a PM should be able to communicate or visualize a working prototype, a rough sketch on a napkin, or a resounding pitch of the product.

This also requires out of the box thinking to solve problems in a refreshing way.

Analytical

PM's need to be able to wear multiple hats or be masters of varying entrepreneurial skills.

We also need to be able to zoom in or go really deep when we need to uncover quantitative and qualitative data insights.

A PM that is able to generate their own data reports and/or query for the data they need may be able to reach decisions more quickly.

In addition to zooming in, a successful PM will know when to zoom out and pivot/reset his/her strategy in line with the specific analyses they have uncovered.

Be wary of those who try to manipulate data for their own advancement. And do recognize that there are multiple ways of seeing data and how it is presented.

When building something new, there may be little data so think about the data you need to cultivate such as from A/B testing (control and tests against the control) or customer validation testing.

Strategic POV (point of view)

PM's require a strategic view of their product and where it is headed such as with a roadmap. Passion for the strategy will help to steer the momentum for the overall product roadmap.

Zoom out to see the forest (versus the trees) in order to communicate the overall product and where it is headed in line with your vision.

Practice zooming in and out.

Some PMs are stronger zooming in and some are stronger zooming out.

Know your strengths and build up your opportunity areas to become invaluable.

Collaborative

PM's generally don't build and scale products via 'Me, Myself, and I'. Ego-driven development would likely increase re-work. Expensive time and cost can be saved just by listening to customers and colleagues.

Collaborative PM's bring the best out of their cross-functional team(s) whether it is from developers, data scientists, A/B testers, and/or UX designers.

Customers and also stakeholders can also contribute to the collaboration.

When the customer need and data resonate with the collective team, the PM can help motivate the best out of their team to build the product.

Tenacity

PM's need to fail fast to get to a successful product. That means being able to iterate and being able to pivot when needed to get to success as quickly as possible.

PM's need to push through painful moments as learning lessons and encourage the team to pivot at times to get to breakthroughs.

If customer validations on prototypes fail then a PM with grit will dust off their sleeves and will reset if needed to iterate for the customer.

*See failure as a teacher and an
opportunity to do better.*

Change

PM's who accept change are empowered to become the most agile proponents for the customer.

*They become the cheerleader and also
the team catalyst that embraces change
for the better.*

Always Learning

Successful PMs are always learning from their customers.

PMs who embrace different problem-solving methods and tailor those to meet the needs of their customers often succeed.

With daily advances in technology, PMs who stay on top of digital data/trends, tech advances, and customer insights are able to harness their learnings to help solve for the customer.

Sharing these learnings with the team makes the collective output even stronger.

Authenticity

It is easy to know when someone is being authentic or not. It comes from within and it is genuine.

Being a PM requires authenticity to influence those that may not even report to you.

A PM with an informed point of view, passion, and conviction to solve for the customer will be able to gather support from the team.

It is in the best interest of the PM to motivate their cross-functional team to want to collaborate for best results.

A PM who gives credit to the team and celebrates their collective work will be unlimited in their future endeavors.

Transparency

To embrace the possibilities of product development, it is important to have transparency in the work you are doing to solve problems for the customer. Rarely does anything meaningful get accomplished in silos or without measurement. I think about it as Public Relations for your work.

For stakeholders, it is important to communicate where we are in the product development process and the results we have made.

Often areas of opportunity are related to co-creation with stakeholders and customers.

Managing expectations of stakeholders means to communicate progress and be open to ideas. Review the intended customer experiences along with risks, assumptions and tradeoffs.

This can be in the form of weekly meetings and/or newsletters show casing the hard work the cross-functional team has accomplished.

A little bit of Ta-da!

PMs are empowered to build the right thing and usually need to do it right way. As with any effort, sharing your efforts builds awareness and also opens up the possibilities for valuable feedback.

> *Demos such as with your software development team should be embraced as mini celebrations for the team's hard work.*

I've been known to even perform a semi-acceptable robot dance with team members after a demo. What is your mini celebration dance or activity?

Presentations or meetings should also embrace a show-and-tell type forum where the team is proud to showcase the work they have accomplished.

We PMs are on the stage or on the pitch constantly and we should throw in a bit of Ta-da! to share what we got going with our teams. It may also help to partner up with a Developer or designer from the team to present the team's work (which can also add credibility to the combined effort).

What Tools are helpful for a Product Manager?

Journey mapping

PM's use journey mapping to map out the high and low points of a customer's experience. Journey mapping is also an opportunity to zoom out and see all the ways from beginning to end how a customer interacts with the product.

You can then focus in on an area you decide is important to the journey.

Decide which customer persona example you would like to focus on. Ex, Jane Doe is a 34-year-old mom and is the CFO of her household.

Document each step that Jane Doe goes through and note her emotional state. It may help to print out on giant sheets the actual flow of pages Jane Doe goes through. Or it may help to write out those steps.

Write down the observations on post-its and denote ups and downs for each step. Step back and observe the areas of opportunity.

How might we tackle or eliminate some of Jane Doe's friction points?

Ethnography

Have you ever sat at a public place such as a park bench and just observed?

Journaling helps to understand what is being seen, heard, and observed.

Immersing (Liedtka, 2018) oneself in another environment allows things to come to realization, often those that are not one has noticed before.

What are people doing or not doing?

What emotions such as delight or frustration do you observe?
What are the social rituals or rules that are being adhered to?
What rituals or rules can be modified to solve problems for humans?
Traveling somewhere different (doesn't have to be far way) is also important from time to time. The novelty of a new location makes us process more information and take less shortcuts on what we are used to seeing/noticing.
To unbuckle from familiar surroundings forces us to see things with a fresh perspective.
We have five senses yet rarely take the time to observe with each and all of these senses.
Try to look at familiar place with a fresh perspective. What do you observe?

Theory of mind

Theory of mind is to understand that others have beliefs, desires, intentions, and perspectives that are different from one's own views.

This is a critical skill to have as a PM as we need to,

See the world outside of ourselves to
create solutions and solve problems

I wrote my psychology thesis in relation to Theory of mind and preschool aged children. My then professor Kimberly Cassidy (current Bryn Mawr College President) had given an example of 'Theory of Mind' in class and how children happen upon this. A young child may observe an adult who has bumped their knee on something. The child may react by offering the injured adult with his teddy bear thinking this will help the adult. An older child may react to the injury by offering a band-aid. This is what Theory of Mind is about.

As PMs we are empowered to react or proactively create products that will help humans. To get there though (especially for non-tangible or digital needs) could require stepping back to observe, learn, prototype, and iterate often.

CNVC also published a list of needs (2005) and that can be used as general resource for understanding high level potential needs of the customer.

Customer personas

What are the personas of your customer? Which ones are the hard users or extreme ones? Who is against your product and why? Who is an early adopter and why?

What are the psychographic attributes (refer to Wells, W. (1975). Psychographics: A Critical Review. Journal of Marketing Research) of your customers? It may help to examine their activities, interests, opinions, needs, values, attitudes, and personality traits.

Map out the personas of the customers you wish to learn more about. It may be interesting to then showcase them visually on a wall.

You may even create 2x2's of two different personas and note what you observe. Look at how NYMag.com creates their approval 2x2 matrices for inspiration.

Role playing

It may help to uncover unmet needs through role playing. This involves first identifying the personas of the customer. This can be a fun team exercise as well.

A team member(s) can be the website or app and another team member(s) can be the customer persona(s).

What are the attributes of the persona and the goals of the customer in mind?
What are the jobs to be done?
How does the 'customer' in this role play interact with the product?
What is the intended outcome and potential obstacles or complications?
What emotions exist in this role play exercise?

Co-creation

Behavioral economics includes the studies of humans and how their decisions can be influenced by heuristics.

We as PMs may benefit to recognize when our own heuristics or mental shortcuts come into play when developing solutions for the customer. We may be shortcutting ourselves from more impactful possibilities. Humans are fascinating in the sense that they do not necessarily follow a linear path. From a digital perspective this can mean that touchpoints of a customer may indicate a certain transaction or decision is likely, however there are multiple factors (some that come in

sideways, or are unseen or unvoiced) that can contribute to the final purchase, transaction, or decision (and may not all be rational but emotional or reactive).
That is why I cannot stress enough the value of design thinking and co-creation.

Whether it is engaging with cross functional teams, customers/non-customer, and/or academia, there are multiple perspectives that can be considered for product management activities striving for new value.

Rough sketches or imperfect prototypes are enough to start to gather timely feedback from colleagues or customers.

Instead of spending a lot of expensive design time on a prototype, enlisting various team members (and non-designers) to quickly prototype their envisioned solution could yield multiple possibilities. These possibilities can then be dot-voted on and discussed.

Combining multiple winning prototype aspects into a collective prototype for further testing/validation allows the team to harness the positive effects of co-creation.

Capturing the Customer's Voice

I have seen firsthand the power of video when it comes to capturing the customer's voice. We are often otherwise heavily engaged in bar charts, excel sheets, and presentations.

How often do we observe the customer directly or see/hear from them?

Being able to hear and/or see the customer and capture their experiences firsthand is inarguably a strong source of data for PMs. Whether it is observing their interactions with the digital product, observing customer interviews, or going through customer reviews/feedback this is an important feedback loop for PMs to leverage on an ongoing basis.

Sketchbook/Notebook

As with Frida Kahlo or Leonardo da Vinci, many great thinkers and artists meticulously kept notebooks to write down ideas, sketches, and musings.

Having a place to jot down thoughts and reflections is an important tool for a PM.

In addition to having this space to be creative, it is also a tool for organization and working up to your vision as a PM. I highly recommend bullet journaling for this purpose.

Some possible things to note in your notebook:

What did you observe today? What was interesting about it?
What are some hunches you would like to test?
What sparks interest in you or others that you have noticed?
What has been your Mantra of the day or what will you accomplish?
What is your favorite quote of the day?
What delighted you today?
What is frustrating and how would you solve for it?
Whom did you meet today? What was the conversation about?
What are some authentic moments you have observed or witnessed?
How would you go about making something unfamiliar, familiar or more well-known?

What assumptions/rules have you observed in your daily interactions?
How would you change the rules to alleviate a pain point?

How do I conduct Design Thinking?

There are many ways to conduct design thinking exercises.

Observing and noting as well as conducting customer interviews can provide valuable insights.

Observe and note

Go to the location where your customers might be in action.
Take in the sights and sounds of their surroundings.
Immerse yourself.

What do you notice? What types of actions or question arise from the observation?
Write down your observations in your notebook.

Invite customers to your screen or to a meal

There are many ways to get customer feedback. One of them is to use online tools to capture customer interactions or customer feedback via voice or video.

Or you can invite customers fitting the persona(s) to a meal in a public place and provide a welcoming environment for them to freely share their opinions and comments.

Conduct Customer Research Interviews

When you need in-depth insights about the customer, you will need to plan for conducting research interviews with customer consent.

This requires the creation of the customer personas that you need to focus on for the interview and vetting/recruiting customers that fit these personas.

Use brainstorming or whiteboard sessions to outline the key customer personas you need to recruit for.

Discussion guide (DG)

A discussion guide is a document you outline with questions you need to ask of the customers.

This starts with general warm up questions and then key areas of uncovering needs of the customer. Make sure to craft a DG that will allow the customer to freely express their needs, pains, and comments.

Leading questions will not generate true insights so make sure to vet the DG with another colleague.

Use *"Tell me more"* during the interview and do not react emotionally to customer responses in any way (positive or negative).

There could be contradictions that come out of the feedback and that is something you should try to get more specificity on to go deeper to understand the customer.

Download and Synthesis

This is the step for making and combining ideas to think about your problem differently.

After recruitment and interviews are completed, there needs to be a means to process the information.

This requires sharing or downloading the customer feedback with a few others so that discussions can be had, and insights can be cultivated.

As customer feedback is shared, allow participants to write down what resonates with what they are hearing (one statement or visual per post-it). Once downloads are complete, group post-its into themes. It also important to note artifacts uncovered from the interviews with consent such as photos of customer surroundings and materials the customer shared on his/her experiences.

One example of an interesting customer artifact I have seen was from a meticulous scientist who created mini to-scale 2D paper cutouts of her living room furniture so that she could explore design possibilities in a tactile way.

Customer Insights

As you and a few peers look at the themes or groupings of the customer feedback, have a discussion on the key insights being uncovered.

What is it about this theme makes you want to solve for it?

An insight should be simple enough to understand by itself but also should make a listener delight in it as to respond by saying that is what we need.

What was expected and what was surprising from the findings?

An example of an insight is when I was interviewing customers with shopping habits. There was a couple who always shopped at the store together and in fact considered their Friday night in-store shopping experience as 'date night in the store'. How might we make the in-store experience like 'date night in the store'?

I attended IIT's Institute of Design's bootcamp and insight can be further defined as: <u>how we surface the dynamic tension of the problem to make it actionable</u>.

How Might We's (HMW's) and Hypotheses

According to Stanford's d.School, <u>How might we's</u> (HMW's) can be generated from customer insights so that you can maximize brainstorming results.

Framing in HMW will help peers to activate the insight and set the forum for ideas that will turn into prototypes. Also hypotheses are at the root assumptions that need to be proved or disproved.

Never assume anything and break down hypotheses to generate stronger ones.

Brainstorming

Collective HMW's are laid out on the wall or 6' boards so that rapid brainstorming can occur for maximum output. Establish brainstorm rules that can ensure quantity (versus quality) of ideas at this early stage.

One idea per post it

Build on each other's ideas.
Use "*Yes, and*".
Allow wild ideas. Wild ideas are ok as they will enable lateral thinking that could prove to be valuable.
Don't be devil's advocate and block creativity here in this step.
Make it visual and allow users to draw their idea if they want to.

Announce each idea as you hand over the post it to be put onto the wall. Have the team group ideas by theme for affinity mapping. Use dot voting to narrow in on potential concepts before prototyping.

Make it Visual

One does not need to be a designer to incorporate design thinking.

Just like building a visual wall connecting all the elements of a case on a popular detective TV show, put up pictures, posters, data, stats, prototypes and research around your project on a wall.

Make a vision or inspiration board for the team. Customer personas can also be used on the wall (real names are masked or changed) with photos and descriptors so that the team can immerse themselves with the personas.

"Get to know - Jane Doe' for example can be an area set aside to remind the team that we are building for the customer.

How do we create a Roadmap?

Planning a roadmap is essential to verbalizing your product strategy of what you are building in the future and why.

Secondary benefits to a roadmap are the how and when which delves into project management.

A strong roadmap builds in strategy, customer insights (from research interviews conducted along with third party research) and success metrics. You can use anything from a whiteboard, excel sheet, post-its or online roadmapping tools. The benefit of online roadmapping tools is the ability to access the roadmap anywhere and the ability to filter for different views you want to use to convey your roadmap. The roadmap should speak to the vision and the strategy (what we will do and what we don't do) and be tied to goals/KPIs and objectives.

I like to present chunks of work with HMWs so that it resonates better on what we are solving for the customer. For iteration and bigger initiatives, you may need to work out phases such as 'MVP phase 1' and subsequent phases which are outlined in the roadmap.

You can breakdown what you need in the roadmap with what I would name as the accordion method. Fold a piece of paper into half and then half again. You should have four rows and write the first item or phase at the top row and the end goal or phase at the bottom row. Now think and put down what phases you need in between. After you are good with that, use the pre-folded paper to fold it one more time to create a total of eight rows. Is there anything missing between the top row and the bottom row?

Use HMWs in Epics (the big user story) within Jira to help the software development team understand the customer needs we are solving for. Attach customer data or insights to these Epics to maximize co-creation.

Your backlog should have a collection of prioritized user stories.

User stories are for example in this format,

"As a Customer I need/want ABC so that I can XYZ."

The user story covers the following:

Who is the user story for?
What is the need or want for that user?
What is the impact or benefit?

User stories also have acceptance criteria that outlines what is to be done to complete this story.

The key to stories is that they do not presume the How or the solution. It is up to the team to decide on the How via collaboration and grooming. The PM presents the What.

Each user story should be independent chunks of work that can be delivered on its own and provide value in of itself.

Huge user stories (ones that are pointed high by the team) would benefit from story splitting and can be discussed at grooming. The prioritized user stories will need to be tied together by their Epic.

What is a Strategic Framework?

PMs are often presented with challenges from the business and not all needs come directly from the customer. In this case, it is important for the PM to put his/her MBA hat on and zoom out on the strategic framework for what is being requested to build. We have already stressed the importance of understanding customer needs and validating these needs provide the data for the effort involved.

Having a product vision that is conveyed through the roadmap is helpful for PMs to garner support for their efforts.

Concise business cases on what problem you are trying to solve, the impact envisioned and what is needed for success goes a long way to convey support for your efforts.

Having prototypes with customer data also strengthens the initiative.

In line with <u>Porter's five forces</u>, it may be important to assess the competitive strategy of the product to help determine build or buy situations: How much time do we have to try to build versus buy the solution? What is buildable and also what are the unknowns we can work to uncover? What would provide the longer-term advantage (build versus buy)? Who can we partner with enable scalability? What are the options we haven't uncovered yet?

Per IDEO, design thinking can be seen as a framework that lives within the: <u>intersection of *desirability, viability, and feasibility*</u>

There are many strategic frameworks or tools out there like these where we can simply,

> *Frame the challenge and articulate what we will be doing to solve that challenge.*

Prototype your way to success

Using affinity mapping of the ideas, allow users to sketch multiple rough prototypes on paper or using an online tool accessible by many team members. In the digital world, speed matters.

Just as how important it is to understand the what of the customer need, how you execute also matters. Earlier we also talked about behaviors and co-creation that enable you to maximize your potential as a PM. Prototyping acts as means to brainstorm the concept that arose out of customer insights.

Many fast iterations of prototypes and customer validation sessions will help you get to successful results. Building to learn versus building for perfection speeds up progress. Prototypes are meant to be cheap to create so that we can learn quickly.

Also, egos need to be set aside for co-creation possibilities as the outcome of multiple, diverse team members could provide a richer result. Embrace and collectively push through the discomfort that comes with potential disagreements during your co-creation sessions. When the customer is your compass, the results, customer data and/or feedback will be the thing that will speak for the product itself.

What are some useful Agile Rituals?

Agile is one of many methodologies to manage a software development project.

The rituals of daily stand up, sprint planning, story point grooming, team demos and actionable retrospectives enable a cross-functional team to measure and reinforce the progress of their efforts.

I appreciate the agile method when executed properly to enable all team members to contribute to the collective effort regardless of their role as PM, Scrum Master, Developer, UX Design, or Tester.

The PM's contribution in sprint planning is to bring prioritized stories in line with roadmap to the team for commitment to the sprint (based on the ongoing capacity/velocity measured).

Story point grooming is another important ritual for the PM to bring stories and then further refine their stories/requirements with the team. The team then assigns story points based on the size of the work. The team commits to a certain number of stories for the sprint based on their velocity in sprint planning.

Retrospectives after each sprint enable team members to reflect on learnings and express gratitude for team members who stepped up during the sprint.

A story point retrospective is also important for the team to reflect on past work and if there was a delta in the story points committed versus delivered (based on the effort of the work that was ultimately required). This helps the PM grasp the team's sizing for similar work for planning purposes and also helps the team learn and refine their capacity.

It is important to reinforce retrospective learnings with committed actions that will further grow the team to increase their collaboration, velocity and outcomes.

Team values

Just as having a strategy is important for the business, the agile team needs to be grounded in,

Team values of what is important to the team in our ways of working with each other

These are the ground rules that the team establishes together.

This helps to maximize collective output and acts as a team compass for working well with each other.

Having a safe and transparent environment to voice opinions, concerns, or provide valuable feedback to each other enables better outcomes and growth collectively.

What is it I am hearing (perhaps over and over again)?

Feedback is a valuable tool whether it comes from the customer, stakeholder or colleague.

For growth there is a constant need to adapt to change and the need to challenge ourselves to make improvements. In order for PMs to refine their craft it is worth asking for continuous feedback from the customer, team and various stakeholders. There will always be room for improvement and learning. This also goes into the humility attribute we discussed earlier.

An assertive PM with a strong POV (point of view) is what may have been the norm for traditional product management. However, we need to add a facet of humility for learning from the customer to be able to solve meaningful problems.
Rich opportunities come from cross-collaboration with diverse individuals.

How might we step away from ego or silo driven development to customer needs driven development? For example, let's play a simple game. I am craving something new to eat and for the purposes of the game I am unable to share what it is.

Do you know what I want to eat?
Does a cross-functional team know what I want? How would diverse perspectives impact the likeliness of knowing what I want?

How likely would the team know what I want to eat after interviewing my food and dietary needs?

How likely would the team know what I want to eat after giving me some tasting samples, i.e. prototypes?

Embrace Change

Change is inevitable with ever-changing technologies, economies and customer needs. Sometimes change can suddenly occur and without warning.

It may help to acknowledge that change is going to happen.

*Stellar PMs anticipate, plan and be ready
to adapt to change confidently.*

Being an agile PM with the ability to continually learn from our customer(s) and iterate effectively with our team(s) will help to embrace change for success.

Thank You

I am grateful to be able to share this toolkit with you.

I want to thank my children and parents for their unconditional love and support.

Thank you to my colleagues (such as team Jumanji, team Bazinga and many other extended family and friends) who have challenged, supported and inspired me in my path as a PM.

The richness that emerges from teamwork, diversity and collaboration will continue to inspire me on this journey as we work together to solve human problems.

Let's continue to challenge ourselves to be courageously creative with our product building.

Thanks for reading!

Notes and Additional Resources

Throughout my book I have directly linked to sources and/or references as applicable. I have also created this reference list:

Chapter: What is Design Thinking

Antonelli, P., article specific to Liedtka, J. (2013). Rotman on Design: The Best on Design Thinking from Rotman Magazine (Martin R., Martin R., & Christensen K., Eds.). University of Toronto Press. Retrieved May 31, 2020, from www.jstor.org/stable/10.3138/j.ctt5hjvq9

Chapter: What attitudes and behaviors do I need to embody as a PM?

The Second City, How to say "Yes, and" https://www.secondcity.com/how-to-say-yes-and/ (D/L May 31, 2020)

Goleman, Daniel and Boyatzis, Richard E. (2017) Harvard Business Review: Emotional Intelligence Has 12 Elements. Which Do You Need to Work On? https://hbr.org/2017/02/emotional-intelligence-has-12-elements-which-do-you-need-to-work-on (Retrieved May 31, 2020)

Chapter: What Tools are helpful for a Product Manager?

Liedtka, Jeanne (2018) Harvard Business Review: Why Design Thinking Works https://hbr.org/2018/09/why-design-thinking-works (Retrieved May 31, 2020)

Center for Nonviolent Communication Website: www.cnvc.org (2005) Needs Inventory https://www.cnvc.org/training/resource/needs-inventory (Retrieved May 31, 2020)

Wells, W. (1975). Psychographics: A Critical Review. Journal of Marketing Research, 12(2), 196-213. doi:10.2307/3150443 (Retrieved May 31, 2020)

New York Magazine, The Approval Matrix https://nymag.com/tags/the-approval-matrix/ (Retrieved May 31, 2020)

Ryder (2015) How to Bullet Journal https://www.youtube.com/watch?v=fm15cmYU0IM (Retrieved May 31, 2020)

Chapter: How do I conduct Design Thinking?

IIT Institute of Design (2011) Insight Definition from Design Camp https://id.iit.edu/courses/analysis-synthesis-design/ (Retrieved May 31, 2020)

Chapter: How Might We's (HMW's) and Hypotheses

Stanford d. School How Might We Questions https://dschool.stanford.edu/resources/how-might-we-questions (Retrieved May 31, 2020)

Chapter: What is a Strategic Framework?

Porter, Michael E. (2008) Harvard Business Review: The Five Competitive Forces https://hbr.org/2008/01/the-five-competitive-forces-that-shape-strategy (Retrieved May 31, 2020)

IDEO Design Thinking Defined https://designthinking.ideo.com/ (Retrieved May 31, 2020)

Feel free to reach out to me via opendoorstudies.com if you found this book helpful, if you are interested in coaching or let me know of any resources or topics you want to see included in a follow up.

If you enjoyed this book, I would gratefully appreciate a review on the Amazon site.

Below is also a short list of relevant resources and inspiration you can refer to should you wish to explore more.

What is design thinking?
https://www.ideou.com/blogs/inspiration/what-is-design-thinking

Personas
https://www.interaction-design.org/literature/article/personas-why-and-how-you-should-use-them

Discussion guides for customer interviews
https://www.designkit.org/methods/2

Options for remote customer research
https://www.zdnet.com/article/conducting-customer-research-remotely-tips-tricks-and-resources/

Roadmap tools
https://www.forbes.com/sites/forbesproductgroup/2016/10/31/product-management-tools-of-the-trade/#5c6edcb79a4a

Hooked by Nir Eyal
https://www.nirandfar.com/hooked/

Design Thinking for Innovation by Jeanne Liedtka
https://www.coursera.org/learn/uva-darden-design-thinking-innovation

A Whole New Mind by Daniel Pink
https://www.danpink.com/books/whole-new-mind/

Jira for software development
https://www.atlassian.com/software/jira/guides/use-cases/what-is-jira-used-for#jira-for-software-development-teams

Excel shortcuts
https://support.microsoft.com/en-us/office/keyboard-shortcuts-in-excel-1798d9d5-842a-42b8-9c99-9b7213f0040f?ui=en-us&rs=en-us&ad=us#bkmk_freqwin

SQL queries
https://generalassemb.ly/education/intro-to-sql--2/online

Principles behind Agile Manifesto
https://agilemanifesto.org/principles.html

Jobs to be Done with Clayton Christensen
https://hbr.org/podcast/2020/01/revisiting-jobs-to-be-done-with-clayton-christensen

Why companies need creative leaders
https://www.forbes.com/sites/jasonwingard/2020/05/29/why-companies-need-creative-leaders-in-the-future-of-work/#34129199482a

This Page Left Intentionally Blank